Books should be returned or renewed by the last date above. Renew by phone **03000 41 31 31** or online *www.kent.gov.uk/libs*

OLGA'S OTHER ADVENTURES:

Olga
Follows Her Nose

MICHAEL BOND
ILLUSTRATED BY HANS HELWEG

OXFORD
UNIVERSITY PRESS

OXFORD
UNIVERSITY PRESS

Great Clarendon Street, Oxford OX2 6DP

Oxford University Press is a department of the University of Oxford.
It furthers the University's objective of excellence in research, scholarship,
and education by publishing worldwide. Oxford is a registered trade mark
of Oxford University Press in the UK and in certain other countries

First published 2002
First published in this edition 2022

British Library Cataloguing in Publication Data

Data available

ISBN: 978-0-19-278745-3

1 3 5 7 9 10 8 6 4 2

Cover graphic Shutterstock/Shpak Anton
Cover artwork copyright Catherine Rayner

Printed in Great Britain

Paper used in the production of this book is a natural,
recyclable product made from wood grown in sustainable forests.
The manufacturing process conforms to the environmental
regulations of the country of origin.

CONTENTS

1
Olga Spins a Yarn

'It isn't generally known,' said Olga, 'but guinea-pigs have the most beautiful ankles in the world.'

Noel gave a snort. 'You're telling *me* it isn't generally known. *I've* never heard of it, for a start.'

'That's nothing to go by,' replied Olga, putting on her superior look. She tugged at a large blade of grass that happened to be just in front of her nose. 'There are lots of things cats have never heard of.'

The truth of the matter was she had never

heard the word ankles herself until that morning, but she wasn't going to let the others know that, especially Noel, otherwise she would never hear the last of it. Noel lived up to his name – he was a bit of a Know-all. Besides, she felt sure that whatever ankles were, a guinea-pig's would be the best ever. It stood to reason.

She had woken up to the news that there was something called a "Sports Day" happening at Karen Sawdust's school. The whole family had been up and about much earlier than usual. As far as she could tell, Karen Sawdust was taking part in several races, and both Mr and Mrs Sawdust had promised to join in some of the parents' events.

Mrs Sawdust had entered her name for the mothers' race, and Mr Sawdust was trying his luck in a competition for the best ankles.

In the meantime, having been put out in her run on the lawn to get a bit of fresh air before they left, Olga had been joined by Noel and Graham, the tortoise. Fangio was nowhere to be seen, but that wasn't surprising. Like most

2

hedgehogs, he often slept all through the day, especially during the warm weather.

Noel was busy as usual, airing his views about things in general and Sports Days in particular.

'It happens every year,' he said, knowledgeably. 'Last year Mr Sawdust went in for a knobbly knees contest. He won a propelling pencil. This year it's ankles.'

'I was looking at my knees the other day,' said Graham. 'It helps pass the time. I noticed they're very knobbly. I wonder if they're having another competition this year? I might win a prize if they are.'

'You'll never get there in time,' said Noel. 'It starts this morning. That's why everyone was up early.'

Olga stared at them both. She was beginning to wish she had never boasted about her ankles in the first place when the penny dropped.

Mr Sawdust had been behaving very strangely when he came downstairs to breakfast, lifting up the bottom of his trousers to

3

show everyone the ends of his legs. For some reason he had seemed quite pleased with them, especially when he took his socks off.

All the same, she had been very worried when he trod on one of her Carrot Slims by mistake and began hopping around the room on one leg shouting at everybody. He had narrowly missed landing on Noel. That wouldn't have mattered – it would have served Noel right for being in the way. But several times he had come very close to stepping in her water bowl, and she had been thankful when he put his slippers back on.

'If your ankles are so beautiful,' said Noel, 'show them to us.'

'I'm afraid I can't do that,' said Olga primly. 'Being so beautiful I have to take great care of them. You never know, it might rain and if they get wet they could shrink and that would never do.'

Noel looked up at the cloudless sky. 'There's no fear of that,' he snorted scornfully. 'Anyway, your stomach will keep them dry – it's big enough. I wouldn't risk standing up if I were

4

you. With all that food inside you your ankles might crack under the strain.'

That did it! Olga gobbled down the remains of a dandelion leaf and then drew herself up to her full height.

'There!' she said.

'I can't see them,' said Graham, lowering his head as far as he could. 'Mind you, the grass needs cutting.'

'I've seen better,' yawned Noel, stretching himself out lazily and gazing down at his own legs.

'Where?' said Olga, pretending she hadn't noticed.

Noel didn't even bother to answer.

'Of course,' she continued, 'I can understand

5

you not noticing my ankles before now. That's one of the troubles about being a guinea-pig. There are so many wonderful things about them people don't know which bit to look at first. Their wonderful whiskers . . . their beautiful eyes . . . their fur like silky cream. We aren't like cats. One quick look at a cat and you've seen all there is to see.'

'I don't think I've got any ankles,' said Graham sadly. 'Not many tortoises do. I expect that's why we don't have Sports Days.'

'You'd be better off in the slow bicycle race,' said Noel. 'With a slow bicycle race it's the one who comes in last who wins.'

'Oh, I like the sound of that,' said Graham. 'It sounds just up my street, that does. I'm always last. I think I'll go and get ready – just in case I get called.'

And before the others had a chance to stop him he had turned round and was heading back towards his house.

'I was only joking!' called Noel. 'Your feet would never reach the pedals for a start.'

6

But it was too late. Graham was already halfway up his ramp, and before Noel had time to say any more Mrs Sawdust arrived on the scene and took Olga indoors.

'I've put your lunch out for you,' called Karen Sawdust. 'And I've added a bit extra which you can save until later, just in case we're late getting back.'

'Wheeeee!' squeaked Olga.

'Optimist,' said Mrs Sawdust. 'I can't imagine her saving anything until later.'

'Pessimist,' said Mr Sawdust. 'Don't forget – she's been out on the lawn.'

Lucky me, thought Olga as she stared at the pile of food just inside her dining room.

She normally had her main meal in the evening along with the rest of the family. For lunch she usually made do with a snack, perhaps a baby corn and a French bean or two. Very often she had to fall back on some dried grass which came in a packet and was kept by for emergencies.

But today, laid out on a large lettuce leaf,

there was an array of all her favourite things: freshly sliced carrot, glistening with juice, alongside slices of apple with the outside skin removed in case any of the bits got stuck between her front teeth. She spotted the usual beans and baby sweetcorn, and in amongst them there was even a slice of beetroot.

Sniffing all the goodies one by one, she hardly knew where to begin there was so much.

In the end she decided to start with a piece of broccoli, dragging it to the back of her box for safety.

I think the Sawdust people ought to have a School Sports every day of the week, she thought, as all the goodbyes were said.

It took her a long time to finish off all the food, and it wasn't until she was lying back in her hay wondering what she would do about lunch now that she had eaten everything else, that she gave a thought to her ankles.

Like most guinea-pigs Olga spent a lot of time keeping herself spick and span. You never knew who might come along and pick you up and she liked looking her best. Usually, she began with her face, wetting her front paws and making sure her whiskers and chin were spotlessly clean. But today she thought she would do things the other way round, and begin with her back legs.

However, it wasn't long before she began to wish she had taken Karen Sawdust's advice and saved her extra food until later. The truth was, reaching her ankles wasn't quite as easy as usual. In fact, she almost had to turn herself inside out in order to get her tongue anywhere near them and it was really quite painful.

At one point Noel came in through the pussy flap and caught her at it. 'What are you up to?' he asked. 'I could hear your grunting in the garden.'

'Never you mind,' said Olga.

'Whatever it is,' said Noel, 'I should watch out. You might get stuck like it – then you'll be sorry. You'll need a wheelchair like old Sawdust people have. But don't expect me to push you around. I've got better things to do.' And with that he went back outside again.

Olga wasn't quite sure how or when it happened, but she was so worn out by all her hard work that in no time at all she fell fast asleep.

The first she knew of the Sawdust family arriving back was when she felt herself being picked up and handed round.

'You know,' said Mr Sawdust when it was his turn, 'it's a funny thing – I've never thought about it before, but I think Olga would have done better than me in the most beautiful ankles competition.' He held her up for the others to see. 'In fact, I wouldn't mind betting she would have won it. They really are very elegant.'

Olga preened herself as she stuck her back legs out as far as they would go. 'Wheeeee!' she squeaked. 'Wheeee! Wheeeeeeee! Wheeeeeeeeeee!'

'They do look very shiny,' said Karen Sawdust.

'Not just shiny,' said Mrs Sawdust, '*wet*! If you ask me she's been licking them in her sleep. I think I'd better put her outside in her run so that they can dry off.'

Olga couldn't wait to be taken out into the garden so that she could tell the others her news.

Graham was already waiting outside his house.

'I'm ready if you are!' he called as soon as they were on their own. 'But I've been thinking. I hope they've got a bicycle my size. If my feet don't reach the pedals I might fall off before I start and that won't count. Besides, I might crack my shell and it'll let the water in when it rains.'

Olga opened her mouth as though she was about to say something.

'Don't!' exclaimed Noel. 'In fact, don't even *think* it! I've had enough of your boasting for one day.'

Olga stared at him. 'Boasting?' she repeated. '*Boasting*? You don't know what I was going to say.'

'I think I can guess,' said Noel.

Olga ignored the remark. 'I was simply going to say that I'm sure if Graham and I went in for the slow bicycle race, he would win every time.'

Noel stared at her open-mouthed.

'Thank you very much,' said Graham.

'After all,' said Olga, 'if I'm taking part you won't be able see my legs moving I shall be going so fast, so I couldn't possibly come in last – not even if I tried!'

For once Noel couldn't think of anything to say. Arching his back, he stalked off.

Olga turned to Graham. 'If you like,' she said generously, 'I'll give you a treat and show

you my ankles before they dry off. It will be so
much nicer for you than being in a slow bicycle
race and nowhere near as dangerous.'

2

The Great Jigsaw Puzzle Mystery

'I don't believe it,' said Mr Sawdust. 'Someone's been at my jigsaw puzzle. Just as I was about to take a picture of it too!' Lowering his camera, he stared at the floor to make sure he was seeing alright. 'One of the edge pieces is missing!'

Seeing him get down on his hands and knees and start heading across the room, peering at the carpet as he went, Olga scuttled into the darkest corner of her house. She felt her heart start to beat faster as he drew nearer and nearer.

Oh, dear! she thought. I wonder what he'll say if he finds out I'm sitting on it?

Uncomfortable though it was, she settled down in the hay and pretended to be thinking of other things, which wasn't easy with a lump of cardboard sticking into her stomach.

Luckily, at that moment Mrs Sawdust came into the room.

'It's probably been sucked up by the vacuum cleaner,' she said, addressing Mr Sawdust. 'That's what comes of your leaving it lying on the floor. It's asking for trouble.'

'Sucked up by the vacuum cleaner?' repeated Mr Sawdust. 'We'd better empty the bag before it gets lost altogether. Anyway, it wasn't lying on the floor. I was using that big sheet of plywood I bought specially. It would happen this morning when I wanted to get to the office early. If I leave it where it is goodness knows what will happen to it.'

The voices disappeared into the next room and after a lot of banging and crashing and opening and closing of drawers, Olga heard Mr

Sawdust asking what had happened to something called '*my* screwdriver'.

'You don't need a screwdriver to change the bag on a vacuum cleaner,' said Mrs Sawdust.

'You do now!' said Mr Sawdust gloomily.

Having helped herself to a mouthful of hay, Olga decided to stay where she was for the time being. She was very glad she had, for almost immediately she heard another crash. This time it sounded like breaking china.

'Fancy emptying the bag on to the draining board!' Mrs Sawdust didn't sound best pleased. 'It's gone everywhere . . . '

She broke into a fit of coughing, and even Olga felt a funny tickling at the back of her throat as a small cloud of dust drifted in through the door. She could see it floating in the sun's rays entering through the window. She held her breath for as long as she could, but in the end she had to let go.

'Wheeeeugggggh!' she spluttered.

The sound brought Mrs Sawdust running into the room.

'Now look what you've done!' she cried. 'You've made Olga sneeze. That settles it!'

A familiar pair of legs hurried past. 'I'd better open the French windows for a while to clear the air. I'll have to leave cleaning her out until later.'

'Wheeeeeeeeeeee!' This time Olga managed a very loud squeak.

It didn't go unnoticed.

'Never mind.' Mrs Sawdust propped the doors open with some books. 'It won't be for very long.' And she filled Olga's spare bowl with some of her special dried grass to be going on with.

Olga came out of her hiding place and stared at it. The news that she wasn't going to be cleaned out straight away meant only one thing. Her breakfast would be late arriving! It was a very bad start to the day. There was no knowing what else might go wrong.

She blamed Noel, of course.

Until he had put the idea into her head she had never even heard of a jigsaw puzzle, let alone an edge piece. If it turned out to be what she thought it was, then the missing one would never be the same again. It had tooth marks all over it.

Mr Sawdust had been given a giant jigsaw puzzle for his birthday. It seemed as though it must have been dropped by someone, for when he had first emptied the box there had been a big pile of pieces, and ever since then he had spent most evenings trying to fit them all together.

Olga had caught a glimpse of a picture on the outside of the box showing what the puzzle would look like when it was finished, and as far

as she could make out it was just like the
Sawdust family's own garden. It had the same
pool with its fountain on the patio, and the same
summer house. She could even see a tiny house
just like Graham's. Quite why Mr Sawdust
should go to so much trouble when he only had
to step outside the house to see the real thing
was hard to understand, although many of the
things the Sawdust people did were like that.

The only good thing about it as far as she
could see was that it kept Noel out of the way. It
seemed that once upon a time he had come
rushing in from the garden to escape from a
downpour of rain and had skidded on another
puzzle that Mr Sawdust had just finished
putting together. From that day on he had been
banned from going anywhere near them.

Only the evening before he had passed the
warning on to Olga.

'Just be careful where you walk from now
on,' said Noel, when he saw Mr Sawdust had
finished his new one. 'Especially when you
come out at night like you do. I've seen you. It's

been made from a photograph Mrs Sawdust took of the garden.'

Olga felt Mr Sawdust must be very unlucky with his presents if they kept getting broken, and as soon as he had gone to bed that night she decided to take a closer look.

And that was when the trouble had started. Seen from close to, and by the light of the moon, the picture looked even more lifelike than she had expected. In fact, it was so lifelike, when she came across what she thought was a blade of grass sticking up from the edge of the lawn she couldn't help but give it a passing nibble.

Much to her surprise it had come away from the rest of the picture and try as she might she hadn't been able to put it back where it belonged.

In the end she gave up trying and took it back to her house, hoping no one would notice.

It had been a big disappointment when Mr Sawdust came downstairs in the morning with his camera and saw straight away that it was missing.

Hearing 'goodbyes' being said and the sound of the front door closing as he left for his office, Olga decided to hide the missing piece in one of her tunnels for the time being. With a bit of luck she might be able to put it back in its proper place now that it was daylight.

She was about to come out of the other end of the tunnel when she heard Graham's voice.

'So this is where you live these days,' he said, poking his head round the corner of the French windows. 'I've often wondered.' He gazed at the room. 'I say, it's very big. It's much bigger than mine.'

'Oh, you get used to it,' said Olga grandly. 'Anyway, it isn't all mine. The Sawdust family use it too.'

'Oooh, look!' Graham caught sight of the jigsaw. 'There's a dandelion!' And before Olga could stop him he'd made a grab for it.

'Wheeeeee!' she cried. 'That isn't a dandelion. It's only a picture of one.'

'A picture of one?' repeated Graham. 'No wonder it tastes funny.' He smacked his lips. 'It's very moreish, though, even if it isn't the real thing. I think I might try another.'

'I wouldn't if I were you,' said Olga. She looked round anxiously as Graham set about eating another piece of the puzzle. 'I don't know what Mr Sawdust will say.'

'Grrrachmmph,' said Graham.

'What's going on?' called Fangio as he arrived on the patio to see what all the fuss was about. 'Can anyone have a go?'

Catching sight of the puzzle, he stopped in his tracks. '*Mama mia!*' he cried. 'I like the look of that. It's just what I need for the new house I'm building.'

Fangio was an expert on house building. Like most hedgehogs he owned a lot of property. Most of it was scattered about the garden, under the summer house and such places, but he often spoke about other hideaways he had built.

All of them were built in the usual way. First of all he gathered a lot of wet leaves together. Then he spread them out and sat on them until they'd had time to stick together. Once they had gone hard it was a case of burrowing beneath the sheet and lifting it up to form a roof. It took him a long time and he was always on the lookout for new ideas.

'I expect this will make a very good ceiling,' he announced, after he had cast an expert eye over it. 'It's nice and bendy, so I shan't have to do very much.' And without further ado he stuck his snout under one of the sides and disappeared from view.

For a moment or two the puzzle heaved up and down like giant waves in the middle of an ocean as Fangio pushed his way towards the centre.

Then, all of sudden, there was a noise like a sudden shower of rain on a tin roof as all the pieces broke up. Cascading down about his ears, they ended up in a pile on top of the plywood.

'Oh dear!' Fangio sat blinking in the light. 'Just as I was making myself comfortable!'

'Oh dear is right,' said Noel, as he, too, appeared on the scene. Gazing at the mess, he gave a loud miaow. 'There's going to be trouble over this. You mark my words.'

The others stared at the pile of pieces for a moment or two, then without another word they all quietly went their separate ways.

After he had gone a short distance, Graham disappeared into his shell and pretended he was a stone. Fangio vanished into the shrubbery

taking with him several pieces that had stuck to his prickles. Noel simply melted into the surroundings in the way that cats do.

Olga hurried back into her tunnel. She had work to do. She didn't want Mrs Sawdust to move it before she had destroyed the evidence.

For a while the only sound to be heard was that of chewing. Graham was quite right. Jigsaw pieces might not taste like the real thing, but they were definitely moreish, especially when you hadn't had any breakfast to speak of.

The mystery of how Mr Sawdust's jigsaw puzzle ended up as it had started out – a small mountain of tiny pieces – remained a mystery;

although the Sawdust family talked about it for a long while afterwards.

But to Olga the biggest mystery of all was yet to come.

Some time later Mr Sawdust was given another puzzle. It was exactly the same as the first one, or so he said. Olga couldn't see it, because this time he did it on top of the table.

Then, the strangest thing happened. If she hadn't seen it with her own eyes she wouldn't have believed it. She couldn't wait to tell the others they needn't have worried after all.

No sooner had he finished putting the picture together and taken a photograph, than he broke it all up and put the pieces back in the box!

Sometimes there was simply no telling with the Sawdust people what they would do next. Really, there was no pleasing them. Catch a guinea-pig doing a silly thing like that! thought Olga.

3

How Guinea-pigs Got
Their Rosettes

One morning Olga woke early knowing that she had a story coming on. She couldn't have said what it would be about, but she knew the feeling of old.

Sometimes it just happened, but more often than not it had to do with lots of tiny things that she had seen or heard, all coming together at one and the same time.

It was not unlike one of Mrs Sawdust's cakes. It needed what she called "all the right ingredients". Leave just one thing out and it didn't taste at all as it should. Not that Olga knew much about cakes. She had once tried nibbling a piece she found on the floor and it had made her choke.

As she said to Noel afterwards when she saw him sniffing around. 'I would sooner have a dandelion leaf any day of the wheeeeeek!'

When it came to Olga's story, her main ingredients had to do with Mr Sawdust doing some decorating. It seemed that he was on his hands and knees in the room overhead painting something called 'a skirting board'. Every time he stood up and moved to a new bit he started to sing. The trouble was he only knew the first line, so he kept on repeating it: "Maria! Maria . . . Maria . . . Maria . . . ".

He repeated it so often Olga gave up admiring the reflection of her rosettes in the water bowl and buried her head under what was left of the hay.

Even Karen Sawdust began complaining. 'It wouldn't be so bad if Daddy knew some more words,' she said. 'Or picked a different song. It's as old as the year dot and it's putting me off my homework.'

'Shush!' said Mrs Sawdust. 'You don't want to rub your father up the wrong way. He'll never get the job done if you do. Besides, I've no hot water and he's promised to look at the boiler.'

Soon afterwards she went into the kitchen and shut the door, leaving Olga on her own, her mind bubbling over with ideas as she put two and two together and ended up with goodness knows how many.

All I need, she thought, is someone to tell my story *to*.

At that very moment the pussy flap went bang and Noel came running in from the garden.

'Guess what,' he announced. 'There's a giant bird sitting on top of our roof.'

Olga ignored the remark as best she could. Given half a chance Noel would end up telling *her* a story and that would never do.

'It had great long legs,' he said. 'And it was

29

staring down at me with big beady eyes. Bigger
than yours and that's saying something.'

'I shouldn't worry,' sniffed Olga. 'If they're
as good as mine it won't want to come any closer
to you. Not if it's got any sense. Anyway, you can
tell me about it later. I'll try and slot you in,' she
added, using a phrase she'd once heard Mr
Sawdust use on the telephone.

'I'll slot *you* in if you're not careful,' said
Noel darkly. '*If* I can find one wide enough.
Then you'll be sorry.'

'I don't know what you mean,' said Olga,

collecting her thoughts together. 'As a matter of fact, I was about to tell you a story.'

'Not another one,' groaned Noel. He looked as though he wished he'd stayed in the garden.

'This one happened a long, long time ago,' said Olga. 'It was in the year dot BR, and . . . '

'Dot BR?' Noel sat down again, interested in spite of himself. 'When was that?'

'Before Rosettes, of course,' said Olga. 'I thought everyone knew that! I've probably told you before about a country called Barsance,' she continued. 'If you remember, it used to be part of Peru, where all the best guinea-pigs come from, but it broke off one night during a terrible storm and because it was so small there was only room for one of everything.'

'Why was it called Barsance?' asked Noel suspiciously. 'I've forgotten.'

Olga gathered her thoughts for a second or two. 'Because,' she said, 'the man whose land it had broken away from was so surprised he shouted out the very first word that came into his mind. "Oh, Barsance!" he cried. "There

goes my back garden!" Anyway, in time
Barsance – as it came to be known from that
moment on – was ruled over by a very fierce
king. And he wasn't just fierce, he was big with
it. In fact, he was so big that when he laughed

the whole kingdom shook. And when he got in
a bad mood and snorted everything that wasn't
tied down used to rise up in the air. The royal
dustbins ... waste paper ... the one and only
cat ... They all got blown away and were never

seen again. The only good thing about him was that he loved guinea-pigs. He couldn't get enough of them. "Bring me more guinea-pigs!" he used to shout. "What's keeping you?"'

'If there was only one of everything else,' said Noel suspiciously, 'why did he want more guinea-pigs?'

'Because,' said Olga patiently, 'he couldn't help himself. In the beginning he only meant to have one, but somehow he couldn't stop. Besides, unlike the cat, he found them very useful about the palace.'

'Doing what?' demanded Noel.

'Well,' said Olga, 'being low down on the ground they could reach the parts of his palace other animals couldn't. They used to look for his collar studs under the bed when he got up in the morning. And when he was dressed they even tied his shoelaces for him. The king was very fat, you see, so he couldn't bend down. His one and only servant was always banging his head against the king's stomach when he tried to tie them and that made him cross.

'Others used to keep the royal carpets clean by picking up all the crumbs after he'd had his breakfast. The king, who didn't like other people making a noise, said the guinea-pigs were better than his one and only vacuum cleaner and much, much quieter. After breakfast teams of them used to go out and nibble the grass on the royal lawn. They kept it looking like a billiard table. When the sea was calm people used to come over from Peru just to see it.

'And every year, when it was time for spring cleaning, they set to work painting the royal skirting board. When it was time for bed, they untied the king's shoelaces for him, and after they had tucked him in they used to sing him a lullaby.

'Then one day the one and only boiler in the castle broke down and because the King had only one sheet and one blanket he got very cold at night. Once again, the guinea-pigs came to his rescue. He took to having a dozen or so in his bed to keep his feet warm. They all had a hot drink before climbing in and he used to say that because of their lovely fur they made the best hot-water bottles in the whole wide world.

'To show how grateful he was he gave them some special hay that was grown on the royal farm. It had the strongest, sweetest smell imaginable. Not only that, but it was wonderful to eat. In fact, that was the trouble. One night two of them smuggled some in to the king's bedroom in case they got hungry during the night, and because it was very hot under the bedclothes the hay began to smell even more.

'That made them sneeze and soon others joined in; first one and then another, until in no time at all they were all sneezing and the royal bed began to shake. Then the king himself started to sneeze. "Aaaaaaaaatishoooooo!" he

36

went. "Aaaatishoooooo! Aaaatishoooooo! Aaaatishoooooooooooo!"

'They were some of the loudest sneezes it was possible to imagine. They were so loud the whole palace shook and the sound could be heard all over Peru. Well, I expect you can guess what happened next. The king's bed collapsed! His one and only sheet went one way, his one and only blanket went another, and there were pigs scurrying to and fro in all directions.

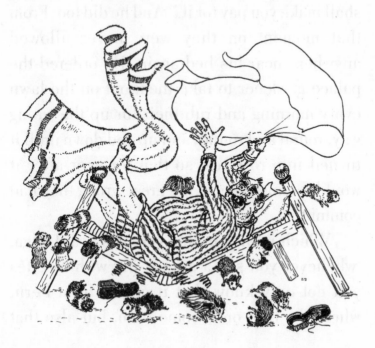

' "Fetch me my shoes!" bellowed the king. "Fetch me my shoes! And be quick about it." It was still pitch dark and in the confusion those pigs whose job it was to look after the king's laces, tied them together by mistake. When he tried to walk he fell over with a great crash and he gave his loudest roar ever as he lay on the floor with his legs in the air.

' "That settles it!" he cried. "You pigs have really rubbed me up the wrong way tonight. I shall make you pay for it." And he did too! From that moment on they were never allowed anywhere near his bed again. He ordered the palace gardener to take them out on the lawn every morning and rub their fur up the wrong way; round and round, and up and down until it turned into rosettes, so that for ever after it would remind them of the great wrong they had committed.

'Which is why, to this very day,' said Olga, 'whenever you see a guinea-pig with rosettes you not only know that it comes from Peru, where the best ones come from, but also that you should always be especially kind to it and help it in every way possible. For instance . . . ' She felt quite empty after all the talking. 'For instance, if you hear one go "Wheeeeeeeee!" you should bring it grass and dandelions and other nice things for it to eat. The more rosettes a guinea-pig has the more it must have suffered,' she went on. 'Karen Sawdust says I've got more rosettes than there are days in the *wheeeeek*, so I expect I need looking after more than most!'

'Schreooooowwww!' Noel lifted up his head in disgust and made a noise that was half miaow and half snort. 'I don't think much of that as a story!'

He was about to go back out in the garden when he thought better of it and stalked out of the room instead, waving his tail angrily to and fro.

He wasn't gone very long before he came back in again.

He looked at Olga suspiciously. 'I seem to remember,' he said, 'you once told me that guinea-pigs got their rosettes as a reward for helping to rescue the king's daughter so that she could marry a handsome prince.'

It wasn't often that Olga was lost for words, but for a moment or two she had to pretend she was busy with her bowl of oats. That was the only trouble with telling stories – there were times when you couldn't help forgetting what had gone before.

Then, hearing a movement overhead, she recovered.

'You must have dreamt it,' she said, after a suitable pause. 'You'll be telling me next your name's Noel, when we all know it's Maria.'

Her timing couldn't have been better.

She had hardly finished when the words 'Maria! Maria . . . Maria . . . Maria . . .' came floating down the stairs.

'I think you're being called,' said Olga casually. 'If I were you I'd hurry.'

A wild look came into Noel's eyes, and this time he really did disappear. Braving the bird outside, he shot out through his pussy flap like a startled rabbit.

40

Olga went back to her oats bowl. She gave a deep sigh of contentment. There was nothing she liked better than telling a story, especially when it had a happy ending. She doubted if even one of Mrs Sawdust's best cakes could have worked quite so well.

One way and another it had been a very good start to the day.

4

Olga's Nasty Experience

From time to time, Olga went 'potty'. At least, that's what Karen Sawdust called it, and although nobody else could think of a better word to describe what happened, Mrs Sawdust did sometimes wonder if perhaps it only happened when there was a full moon. She often meant to look in her diary, but somehow she never did.

Be that as it may, from a standing start, and without the slightest warning, Olga would occasionally emerge from her house at high speed. Thundering straight through her tunnels, she would then tear round the table several times, in and out of feet and chair legs, doing figures-of-eight and various other manoeuvres, until she decided she'd had enough. At which point she would go back to where she had started from and sit there, looking as though butter wouldn't melt in her mouth.

Whether she had planned the route beforehand or whether it was all down to split-second timing no one ever knew, but it was a conversation stopper whenever it happened, and it was never the same twice over. For someone so small, it could also be very noisy.

Mr Sawdust often likened it to a group of wild Cossack horsemen charging across the Russian Steppes, although since Mrs Sawdust regularly vacuumed the carpet it was without the cloud of dust that usually followed in their wake.

If Olga had worn trousers, Karen would have said she had ants in her pants.

As it was, it became yet another one of life's unsolved mysteries. In any case, for the time being the Sawdust family had other things to think about.

Noel wasn't the only one to have seen a heron on the roof of their house. The very next morning, which happened to be a Saturday when everyone was home for the weekend, Karen Sawdust came downstairs to breakfast carrying a large book.

'I've been reading up about them,' she said. 'Listen to this . . . They have a very long neck . . . well, I knew *that* . . . what I didn't know is that because of the way the bones inside it are joined together they can only bend it up or down – they can't make it go sideways. That's why, when they're sitting, they make their neck go into a shape like the letter S. It's so that their head can rest between their shoulder blades.'

'I see Middlesex are doing better this season,' said Mr Sawdust from behind his newspaper. 'They had a good crowd at Lord's yesterday.'

'Cricket!' Karen gave a sigh and turned to her mother. 'It also says that herons can actually fly with their head tucked in that way. They only extend it when they want to seize their prey. With their wings outstretched they look very graceful as they glide through the air, but beware – often it's only the quiet before the storm. They can suddenly drop like a stone, descending like a dive-bomber as they home in on their target.'

'Yes, dear, very interesting,' said Mrs Sawdust vaguely, 'but I should get on with your breakfast otherwise it'll be cold.' She sounded flustered as she disappeared into the kitchen.

Karen gave another sigh, buttered her toast, then looked down at the floor.

'I bet you'd be interested in this bit, Olga,' she said. 'It's to do with food. Heron's food consists mainly of fish and frogs – although if they're hungry they don't mind what they eat. They can stay still for ages before they strike, but when they do it's very quick. They take careful aim and their long beak goes straight to its target.'

Olga didn't like the sound of that at all.

Even though the book didn't mention guinea-pigs she wished she hadn't listened, and she had a larger than usual nibble of her oats, in case it happened to be her last.

'Don't worry,' said Karen, catching sight of the worried look on her face. 'It goes on to say that once a heron has made a catch it swallows it whole. You'll be quite safe. You wouldn't get past its Adam's apple.'

'Does your book say anything about any of the other animals?' asked Mrs Sawdust, as she came back into the room.

Karen took a quick look at the index. 'There are a couple of pages about tortoises. More or less the same amount about hedgehogs . . . a whole chapter on cats . . . but there's no mention of guinea-pigs . . . '

Noel, of course, *would* choose that moment to saunter past. He didn't actually say anything, but he was wearing his 'I'm not surprised' look.

'Wheeeee!' called Olga. 'I expect it's because there's so much to say about us we need a special book all to ourselves.'

46

There was an answering bang from the pussy flap.

'I think Noel's got the right idea,' said Karen, a bit later on after breakfast. Getting down on her knees, she gathered Olga up. 'It's much too nice a day to stay cooped up indoors.'

After all she had heard about herons, Olga wasn't so sure about that, but she didn't have any choice in the matter, and in any case while she was in Karen's hands she felt perfectly safe.

As they went outside into the garden she sniffed the morning air. It did have a lovely fresh smell to it, and there was hardly a breath of wind to ruffle her whiskers. Looking up towards the roof as they crossed the patio, she couldn't see anything unusual. In fact, it was so quiet and peaceful she could have been a part of Mr Sawdust's jigsaw puzzle.

Passing the pond, she glimpsed a flash of colour as one of the goldfish broke the surface – she wasn't sure if it was George or Margaret, it was hard to tell them apart – and anyway it disappeared again as quickly as it had come.

Venables, the toad, was sunbathing near the fountain; the top of his head peeping out from the middle of a clump of weed as he kept a watchful eye open for food. He was so still he might almost have been made of stone himself. A dragonfly hovered over the water before realizing he was there, and wisely took off again.

Olga's nose gave another twitch as they made their way under the pergola and she caught the smell of roses. Hearing them coming, a squirrel made a dive for the mulberry tree, clung to the nearest branch like a trapeze artist for a moment or two, then vanished.

There was no sign of Graham. But in the summer he often found himself a sunny patch in one of the flower-beds, merging in with the foliage for hours on end.

Karen Sawdust found a suitable spot in the middle of the lawn for Olga's run, manoeuvred it into place with one hand, placed Olga carefully inside the box at one end, then gently lowered it back down on to the ground.

Having made sure part of it was in the shade in case it got too hot, she left her to it.

Olga waited a moment or two until all was quiet before venturing out onto the grass, then she made her way towards the far end of the run where there was a particularly succulent-looking dandelion. Having made short work of it, she turned her attention to the grass.

It reminded her of the story she had told Noel about the guinea-pigs in Barsance and of the time when they had kept the royal lawn looking as smooth as a billiard table. Really, there were moments when living with the Sawdust family was very similar.

In her mind's eye she could picture it all. How the pigs would start at one end of the lawn and go backwards and forwards – just like Mr Sawdust with his mower, only not so noisy, of course, and *much* more thorough.

In fact . . . talking of noises . . . Olga stopped eating for a moment and pricked up her ears as she heard a familiar snuffling and grunting heading in her direction through the flower bed.

'I can hear you!' she called. 'I can hear your nose. *And*,' she added, as some leaves parted and something small, black, and shiny peeped out at her. 'I can see it. You want to watch out. Mr Sawdust might cut it off with his clippers one day.'

'*Mama Mia!*' Fangio burst through into the open. 'I wouldn't like that. I don't know what I would do without my nose.'

'It's what he calls "dead-heading",' said Olga.

'I wouldn't like to be dead-headed either,'

said Fangio. 'Mind you, I don't know what I would do without my hear-sight, especially when I've been digging and my nose gets blocked. I can hear a caterpillar munching from as far away as you are. I've caught many a beetle that way.'

'It's all very well for you hedgehogs,' said Olga. 'Just because you've got prickles you don't care how much noise you . . .'

'Shh!' said Fangio. 'Hear that?'

'What?' asked Olga.

'There's a worm going past. It sounds like a biggy. You should try it some time – listening instead of talking. You ought to be able to hear lots of things going on with ears your size.'

'Ears my size?' repeated Olga. 'What do you mean?'

'I'm not telling you who told me,' said Fangio, 'but Noel thinks they're bigger than his pussy flap. He says you can hear a refrigerator door being opened from the next room. I'm surprised you can't hear that worm. Anyway, I must go. *Arrivederci*.' And with that he started snuffling again and went on his way leaving Olga feeling very upset.

Big ears! she thought. BIG EARS! Anyway, who wants to listen to a lot of caterpillars and worms? I expect if I wanted to I would be able to hear much more interesting things!

Having first looked around to make sure she wasn't being watched, she put her head to the ground.

It felt lovely and cool, and although she wasn't able to put both of her ears down at once, she did feel a tickle in the one nearest the earth. She was even able to take a quick nibble of the grass while she listened.

She wasn't at all sure what a worm would

sound like when it was at home, and although for a moment she thought she heard some tiny footsteps, most of the noise came from her own chewing.

Suddenly her heart almost stopped beating as all manner of things happened at once. First there was a rush of air and a kind of flapping noise, not unlike that made by Mrs Sawdust's washing when it was hanging out to dry on a windy day.

Then a shadow fell across the roof of her run and everything went dark.

At the same time the tickling in her ears grew stronger and stronger until she could hardly bear it.

Olga jumped to her feet and made a dash for the safety of her box. In her panic she first of all went the wrong way and rebounded off the wire netting at the end of her run.

Then she tore back the way she had come. Almost immediately she rushed out of her box and started running round and round in circles.

'Wheeeee! Wheeeeeeeeeee! Wheeeeeee-eeeeeeeee!' she shrieked, as she paused for a brief moment to scratch her ear. 'Help! Wheeeeee! Wheeeeeeee! Wheeeeeeeeeeeeeee!'

'Look!' cried Mr Sawdust from inside the house as he saw what was going on. 'Everybody . . . come quickly. Olga's having one of her attacks!'

Mrs Sawdust and Karen followed hard on his heels as he rushed through the kitchen and out into the garden.

Even Graham was woken by the commotion. 'I'm coming!' he called. 'I'm coming!'

'Did you see it?' cried Karen, as a large shape disappeared over the rooftops. 'Did you see it?'

'Olga,' said Mrs Sawdust, 'you're a very brave pig. Fancy fighting off a great bird like that.'

'Most pigs seeing a heron about to land on top of them would have had a heart attack,' agreed Karen. She upended Olga's run, picked her up and gave her a cuddle.

'I don't suppose it was after Olga,' said Mr Sawdust. 'More likely the goldfish. Olga rushing around like she did must have frightened it off at the last moment. I doubt if we shall see it again for a while.'

Noel, who had turned tail as soon as he saw the heron swooping down, was the last on the scene. He didn't actually say anything, but Olga could see that he was impressed.

'Look!' Karen Sawdust was about to kiss the top of Olga's head when she gave a sudden cry. 'It's no wonder Olga was running round and round in circles.'

She held a finger up for everyone to see, then shook it to dislodge a small black object on the end. 'She may not have had ants in her pants, but she had one in her ear!'

Noel pricked up his own two ears.

'An *ant*!' He gave a miaow, halfway between a cry of scorn and 'I might have known'. 'I expect it thought it was going somewhere interesting. It must have been disappointed when it found there was nothing to see.'

'Nothing to see!' Olga indignantly peered out from inside the crook of Karen Sawdust's arm where she had gone for safety. 'Nothing to see! Wheeeeee!'

For a brief moment she was lost for words. Then she remembered what Graham had said earlier. 'That's why my ears are the size they are,' she said. 'There's so much to see inside them I expect when I was made they had a job fitting it all in. I'll tell you a story about them if you like.'

But Noel had gone on his way. So, too, had Graham. In fact, Olga's audience was vanishing almost as quickly as the heron had only moments before.

Oh, well, she thought to herself as Karen carried her back into the house. I certainly shan't waste it. It will make a very good story for a rainy day and I'm sure it will be all the better for keeping!

5

Extra-piggery Perception

'If you ask me,' said Mr Sawdust at breakfast
one morning, 'I think Olga ought to take up
hypnotism. Look at her – she hasn't blinked
once since we sat down.'

'I should be careful,' murmured Mrs
Sawdust. 'There's not much gets past that pig's
ears. She's listening to every word you say. You
might end up like that poor man on television
last night – the one who was put to sleep by the
hypnotist. One stare and he was out like a light.'

'*And* he didn't seem to remember anything about it afterwards,' said Karen Sawdust.

Mr Sawdust looked over his shoulder. 'Come to that,' he said uneasily, 'I don't think I've *ever* seen Olga close her eyes.'

'She doesn't even shut them when she goes to sleep,' agreed Karen. 'Either that or she must wake at the very first sound.'

'It's what's known as extra-piggery perception,' said Mrs Sawdust. 'Guinea-pigs don't like being taken by surprise. They always think the worst is going to happen.'

'You can say that again,' agreed Karen. 'Try creeping up on one from behind and you don't see it for dust. It's a good thing we don't get offended when Olga does it.'

'Better safe than sorry – that's their motto,' said Mrs Sawdust.

Mr Sawdust hastily finished his cup of coffee. 'Of course, they do say the thing to remember about hypnotists is that they can't do it to everyone. They have to find the right person. Someone who is very easily persuaded.'

'If that's true,' said Karen, 'then Olga's got nothing to worry about. You try getting her to do something if she doesn't want to!'

'That's exactly what I mean,' said Mr Sawdust, as Olga went back to foraging in her pot.

Using her nose to find the seeds she liked best, she pushed the ones she didn't like on to the floor. Why they bothered putting the second kind in the packet she would never know. Sorting them out took up a lot of her time, especially as she had to do it all by feel because they were under the end of her nose and she couldn't see them.

She wondered if that was what Mrs Sawdust had meant by extra-piggery perception. If it was, then she was very glad she had it.

Having finished going through the seeds, she began thinking about the television programme.

As far as she had been able to make out, a man with staring eyes had asked a lot of people in a great big room to put their hands behind their head while he was talking. Then, when he

told them to take them away, someone in the front row hadn't been able to do it. He had gone stiff all over.

In fact, he was so stiff that when some other people came along and laid him across the backs of two chairs that had been put close together, he still hadn't moved. He was just like a plank of wood.

Even when the man with the staring eyes sat on him, he still hadn't bent in the middle. It wasn't until the hypnotist had clicked his fingers in front of his eyes that the man had woken up, and as Karen Sawdust said, he still had no idea what had happened to him.

Olga had never seen anything like it before, and by the sound of it neither had the Sawdust family.

After hearing Mr Sawdust talk, Olga

wondered about trying to do the same trick herself, but by that time everyone else had left the table.

There was nothing for it; she would have to wait until she found someone else to experiment on.

As it happened, her chance came soon after breakfast. After she had been cleaned out, Mrs Sawdust put her into the outside run on the lawn while she vacuumed the carpet.

Olga didn't like vacuum cleaners very much. Apart from being noisy, they sucked up everything in their path. She had lost some of her best seeds that way.

She hadn't been on the lawn very long before Graham ambled slowly past taking the morning air.

Olga fixed him with a beady stare. 'Wheeeeee!' she squeaked. 'Your eyelids are looking very heavy this morning.'

'They're always heavy,' said Graham gloomily. 'I have a job keeping them open sometimes.'

'I expect it's because you're feeling sleepy,' said Olga.

'No,' said Graham. 'They're always like it. Besides, I slept all through the winter, so I don't want to go back to bed just yet – it's too early. And another thing – I have to send my eyelids a message first. "Close, eyelids," I say, "and don't open again until next year." The trouble is, once they're shut it's hard to get them open again. I expect that's why we tortoises sleep as long as we do. I've never seen Christmas, you know, not ever. As for having presents like you do . . . '

Olga looked round the garden. Although Graham often went for days on end without saying a word, he had a lot of things bottled up and once he started talking it was hard getting him to stop.

Turning to watch a butterfly go past, she caught sight of Noel. He was sitting by the pergola with his back towards her.

'I expect you'd like a nice sleep in the sunshine,' she called. 'I can make you nod off if you like.'

Noel didn't move. In fact, he didn't even bother waving his tail.

Olga took a deep breath. 'Wheeeee!' she squeaked. 'Wheeeee! Wheee! Wheeeeeeeeee!'

It did the trick. Noel nearly leapt out of his skin. Turning round to see where the noise was coming from, he gave a miaow. 'I might have known!'

'I was just saying,' began Olga, 'if you like, I can put you to sleep.'

'I *was* asleep!' said Noel crossly. 'Now you've woken me up!'

'Oh, dear!' said Olga. She thought for a moment. 'I don't suppose you can put your paws on top of your head, can you? If you do I might

be able to make you nod off again. Mrs Sawdust might even put you across some chair backs if you ask her nicely. Then Mr Sawdust can sit on you and see if you bend.'

Noel stared at her. 'What *are* you on about?'

'Mr Sawdust thinks I would be very good at putting people to sleep,' said Olga. 'He said so this morning. All you have to do is look into my eyes. I'll keep them open for you if you like . . . '

'They're always open,' snorted Noel.

'That's because guinea-pigs like it that way,' said Olga. 'Being so round and beautiful, people need time to look at them properly.'

'Beautiful!' exclaimed Noel. 'They look more like two currants. They only stay open because you've got no lids.'

'No lids?' repeated Olga. '*No lids? Wheeeeeeeeee!*'

'All right,' said Noel. 'If you've got lids, close them.'

'They *are* closed,' said Olga. 'I always keep them closed when I'm out of doors so that the sun won't get in – the sun and the flies.'

Olga had once had a fly land on one of her eyes – she couldn't remember which eye it was, but she had been very upset at the time.

'*I* can't see them,' said Noel.

'Neither can I,' agreed Graham, craning his neck to take a closer look.

'There's a reason for that,' explained Olga patiently. 'Guinea-pigs' eyes are so special they can't have any old lids like a cat. They need to be made of the softest, filmiest material it's possible to find; thinner than a butterfly's wings if you can picture that. Why, they're so fine I can't even see them myself most of the time.'

Noel made a choking noise as though he was about to be sick.

'Anyway, I have to be able to see through them so that I know what's going on,' said Olga, firmly. 'It's what's known as extra-piggery perception.'

Noel stared at her. 'Extra-piggery what?' he demanded. 'Where did you hear that?'

Olga ignored the remark. 'It's yet another reason why guinea-pigs' eyes are so big and round. They're made that way so that we can see what's going on behind us . . . '

She broke off as there was a crash from somewhere nearby. It was followed by a groan from Graham.

'Oooooh! That's what comes of trying to close my eyes like you said. I'm not doing that again in a hurry!'

The din brought Mrs Sawdust out into the garden. 'What *is* going on?' she cried, picking up a watering can that was lying across the path.

She looked at Olga. 'If you ask me,' she said, putting two and two together, 'I think it's high time I took a certain pig indoors.'

And without further ado she upended the run, picked Olga up, and went back into the house. Having put her down on the living room carpet out of harm's way, she went upstairs.

Olga sat where she was for a moment or two, getting used to her surroundings. She felt very hard done by, and she was about to go back into her own house when she paused. For some strange reason, the room felt different.

Then she suddenly realized what it was. Mrs Sawdust had left her handbag lying on the floor by the entrance to one of the tunnels.

For a moment Olga felt even more put out. If there was one thing she hated more than anything else, it was change. She liked everything to be in its proper place, otherwise you didn't know where you were. All the same, as she drew near she saw the flap was open and she couldn't resist taking a closer look while she was passing.

The inside of the bag was such a jumble of bits and pieces she couldn't make up her mind what half of them were for, and she was about to go on her way when she stopped dead in her tracks. Fixed to the inside of the flap there was what looked like a picture of herself.

She stared at it for a long time.

There was no doubt about it; whichever way you saw it; backwards, frontwards, sideways, or even upside down, her eyes did have a certain something.

It was easy to see why others might fall under their spell. They probably didn't want to risk missing a single moment. Olga was so pleased with the picture she decided to stay where she was for a while, just gazing at it.

'You know,' said Mrs Sawdust later that same day when they were all sitting round the table again, 'the strangest thing happened this morning. I was getting ready to go out and when I came back downstairs I found Olga fast asleep on the floor by my handbag. I had a terrible job waking her. I nearly sent for the vet I was so worried. She even let me carry her back to her box.'

'But did she have her eyes closed?' asked Mr Sawdust.

Mrs Sawdust put a hand to her mouth. 'Do you know,' she said, 'I was so worried I didn't even notice . . . '

Karen Sawdust gave a cry of excitement. 'It wasn't the handbag with the mirror on the inside flap, was it? Because if it was . . . '

'If it was,' said Mr Sawdust thoughtfully, 'I wonder if Olga saw her reflection and ended up hypnotizing herself? She does stare at things for ages sometimes.'

The Sawdust family went quiet.

'I wouldn't put it past her,' said Karen. 'If she did it must have been a case of pig meeting pig. She still looks a bit dopey.'

'In that case,' said Mr Sawdust, 'there's one sure way of finding out.'

Bending down, he stared into Olga's eyes for a moment or two, then he suddenly leaned forward and snapped his fingers.

Olga didn't so much as blink. She simply stared straight back at him as though he had taken leave of his senses.

'I wish I knew what she's thinking,' said Mr Sawdust, aware of Olga's gaze following him back to his seat.

'Perhaps,' said Mrs Sawdust wisely, 'it's just as well you don't. I can't think what would happen to the world if we always knew what others were thinking. Can you picture it?'

As the room went quiet, Olga joined in trying to picture what it would be like. It took her a long time, but in between carrying on with her oats and several helpings of grass, she decided that perhaps Mrs Sawdust was right and it was a good thing Mr Sawdust hadn't been able to read her thoughts.

For she had been thinking that if only he had

stayed where he was just a little bit longer she might have been able to hypnotize him. Then she could have watched while the others laid him across the back of some chairs and sat on him.

But then again, she might not have been able to make clicking noises with her paw. In which case he could have been stuck like it forever, and he wouldn't have liked that at all.

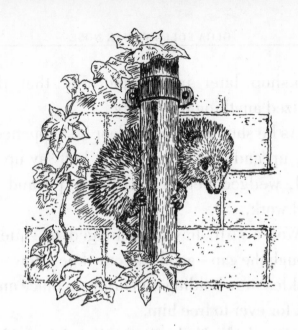

6
Noel Tells a Story

It was a long time before the Sawdust family fully recovered from what they came to think of as 'Black Friday', and it took Olga, Fangio, and Graham even longer to forgive Noel for his part in the affair. For many weeks afterwards his name was even blacker than the fur on his back.

It all began soon after breakfast, but it wasn't until Mr Sawdust went out to his workshop later in the morning that they realized anything was wrong.

As he shut the kitchen door he happened to look up and saw Fangio stuck halfway up the wall, wedged between a drainpipe and the brickwork.

Worse still, having managed to squeeze through the gap – goodness only knew how – his prickles were holding him firmly in place and it took for ever to free him.

After she had helped solve Fangio's problem, Mrs Sawdust went down the garden to check on Graham and found he had barricaded himself inside his house behind a wall of newspapers.

In the meantime, Karen Sawdust looked in on Olga to see how she was getting on and found her crouched in a corner of her run, covered in dirt and looking very sorry for herself indeed.

To make matters worse, Noel had gone missing. It was no wonder they called it 'Black Friday'!

'It must be the heat,' said Mrs Sawdust. 'It's affecting us all.'

Olga would have agreed with that! She couldn't remember ever having felt quite so hot before in the whole of her life.

The sigh she had given when she was first put in her run that morning had said it all, and it would have served as a warning to the Sawdust family if only they had been there to hear it.

She had been finding it hard to breathe, and what had started off as a low rumble deep down inside her came out as a sigh; and not just any old sigh, but one of the best she had ever made. In fact, it was so good she tried it out again on Noel when he went past.

'I've been thinking,' said Olga. 'It's very nice being a guinea-pig and having the most wonderful fur in the world, and I know I shouldn't grumble when there are so many other creatures – like cats – who have to make do with what they've got, but I do sometimes wish mine wasn't quite so thick.'

She thought about it a moment longer. 'It probably comes from being stroked so much. People can't help themselves, you know.

Whenever they see a guinea-pig, they simply have to stroke it, and I suppose the more their fur gets stroked the thicker it gets. I'll tell you a story about it if you like,' she added.

Olga didn't have anything in mind, but she felt sure an idea would come to her once she started. It might even be about a guinea-pig whose fur became so thick it disappeared from view altogether and was never seen again. Except, of course, although that might please Noel, it wouldn't be what she would call a happy ending.

Olga liked stories with happy endings.

Noel gave a snort. 'I'd like to tell *you* a story for a change,' he said, 'and mine will be better than all of yours put together, because mine happens to be true. It's not your fur that's making you feel hot,' he began. 'It's global warming! It has to do with there being too many cars on the roads and . . . and . . . and . . .'

Noel prided himself on knowing about things long before any of the other animals, especially when it was bad news, but he wasn't always very good on details, and his voice trailed away as he tried to remember what else he'd heard about global warming.

'Anyway,' he went on hurriedly before Olga had a chance to butt in, 'there are too many cars on the roads and all the smoke from them has burnt a big hole in the sky. It's letting the clean air out and bad air in. That means the weather has become topsy-turvy. Nothing is the same any more. It's either too hot or it's too cold, or else it's too wet or it's too dry.'

Olga stopped eating for a moment and gazed up through the wire netting roof of her run. Now that Noel mentioned it, she'd heard the Sawdust family grumbling a lot about the weather just lately. They kept looking out of the window, hoping for a storm to clear the air, but somehow it never happened.

Also, she had to admit the grass didn't taste anywhere near as nice as usual. It was no longer green; in fact, it was beginning to look more the colour of her oats bowl.

'It's no good your looking for the hole,' said

Noel, getting a bit of his own back. 'It's much too far away. You'd need to stand on a box. I've got a job seeing it myself at times.'

'I don't see why guinea-pigs should suffer just because Sawdust people use their cars all the time instead of walking,' said Olga plaintively.

Noel sniffed. 'If guinea-pigs could drive it would be even worse. I wouldn't like to be in a car with you at the wheel. If you saw another one coming towards you, you'd turn tail and drive back home as fast as you could. Except, of course, you haven't got a tail so you would have to stay where you were.

'The roads would be full of cars pointing in the wrong direction. It would be like those pictures you see on television, when all the traffic gets stuck and it can't move. It's what they call "gridlock". I expect if guinea-pigs could drive it would be called "pig lock". Think of the shrieking that would go on if that happened. Nobody would be able to hear themselves think.'

Olga pretended she wasn't listening.

'Anyway,' said Noel, 'you should know all about global warming.'

'What do you mean?' asked Olga.

'Because you're so fat you look like a globe,' replied Noel bluntly. 'That's what comes of eating so much. Even when you're outside you don't just sit on the grass thinking how lucky you are to have something nice to lie on – you eat it! If it were left to guinea-pigs there wouldn't be any globe left to get warm. You'd gobble it up between you all.'

'Ho! Ho! Ho!' roared Graham, who happened to be going past at that moment. 'That's a good one, that is. I must remember that.'

'There's another thing about global warming,' said Noel. He looked round the garden to make sure they were alone. 'I don't want to worry you, but there's something called a polar ice-cap.'

'What's that?' asked Olga, becoming interested again in spite of herself. 'Is it anything like the cap Mr Sawdust wears when he's gardening?'

'No,' said Noel. 'It's much bigger than that. It's like a gi-normous ice-cube and it's starting to melt. And because it's right at the top of the world, the water will have nowhere to go, so it will all run down the sides. That means it won't be long before it gets here and everything will be flooded.'

'Wheeeeeeeeeee!' cried Olga in alarm.

'*Mama mia!*' There was an answering cry from Fangio in the shrubbery. He'd also been having trouble getting to sleep and from early morning he had been out looking for a shady spot that stayed where it was long enough for him to doze off.

Graham joined in. 'I don't like the sound of that,' he said. 'I don't like the sound of it at all. I wish you hadn't told me.'

'*Arrivederci!*' called Fangio. There was a rustle of dried leaves as he made his way deeper into the undergrowth. 'Tell me when it's all right to come out, Olgi Polg.'

'I'm off to higher ground,' said Graham, heading back towards his ramp.

'I wouldn't fancy his chances in that house of his,' murmured Noel, as soon as he was out of sight. 'The first wave will sweep it away. Who knows where he'll end up.'

He turned to Olga and looked her up and down. 'As for you letting Fangio know when it's

safe to come out – I expect you'll be one of the first to go, being low on the ground. I'm not sure how long a guinea-pig can stay afloat. Especially with all that fur you keep boasting about.

'Of course,' he continued, 'being a cat, I've no need to worry. All I need do is find the right tree and climb up to the very top. Then I shall simply sit there along with all the other cats until the water goes away. I think . . .'

Noel's voice trailed away. Having started off by saying he didn't want to worry everyone else, he was beginning to look uneasy himself. He glanced anxiously up at the sky.

'I think we're in for a storm,' he said, as he turned to go. 'I can feel it in my whiskers.'

'Come back!' called Olga. 'You haven't finished your story. Has it got a happy ending?'

But it was too late. He had already disappeared.

She stared at the spot where he had been. It was all very well for Noel. He could go anywhere he liked in the world. He could climb trees. He could come and go through his pussy flap. He could even visit the North Pole and see how it was getting on if he wanted to. Guinea-pigs couldn't go anywhere unless someone took them.

She was about to seek safety in the box at the end of her run when she happened to look down and spotted something she hadn't noticed before.

Halfway along one side – the side nearest to

83

the flower bed – there was a gap between the wooden frame and the ground.

It was only a small gap because Mr Sawdust went to a lot of trouble rolling his lawn regularly in order to keep it nice and level. In fact, it was so small she wouldn't normally have seen it, and it was much too tiny for anything to get underneath it and attack her. It probably only looked worse because the grass was so dry. But . . . and it was a VERY BIG BUT . . . it was certainly large enough to let the water in if the garden did get flooded.

Olga eyed it nervously. She looked round the garden. Everything had suddenly gone very quiet.

Pressing her nose up against the wire netting she opened her mouth and uttered several loud cries: 'Help!' she squeaked. 'Wheeeeeee! Wheeeeeeee! Wheeeeeeeeeeeee!'

But she might just as well have saved her breath. Not so much as a leaf stirred.

This time her sigh was longer and even more heart-felt than before.

Having decided it was every animal for itself in this world, she took a deep breath and set to work; scratching, digging, pushing, shoving, packing the earth into place as fast as she could go . . . There was no time to lose!

Which was when Karen Sawdust found her. Except by then Olga had done quite enough digging for one day and she was curled up waiting for the worst to happen.

'Olga! What *has* been going on?' Karen upended the run and picked her up. 'Just look at the mess you're in! I don't know what Daddy will say when he sees what you've done to his lawn, but we'll worry about that later.'

She carried Olga into the kitchen and put her on the draining board. 'I know one thing you need before you're very much older. That's a good bath!'

Sprinkling some liquid shampoo into the sink, she turned on both taps and as the water began to rise, tested it carefully to make sure it was neither too hot nor too cold. Then she carefully lowered Olga into the middle of a pile of bubbles, holding her up in case any soap went into her eyes.

In no time at all the water turned black. Olga sat very still and watched as bits of dry grass began floating past the end of her nose.

Next, Karen laid a warm towel across her lap, made a hollow in the middle, then she turned on an electric hair drier.

Olga lay back with her legs in the air, tired but happy. There was nothing like being in your own home. She not only felt squeaky clean, but she also felt very pleased with herself. If everyone did as she had done and filled up just one hole every day they would soon put an end to global warming.

'Cats!' Mr Sawdust broke into her thoughts

as he came into the house. 'Fancy getting stuck up a tree! I wondered where the miaows were coming from.'

'We'd better call the fire brigade,' said Mrs Sawdust reaching for the telephone.

'They won't be best pleased,' said Mr Sawdust. 'It's started to rain. That's all we need!'

Olga pricked up her ears. Cats! Fire brigade! She remembered the Sawdust family having to call the fire brigade out once before when Noel had got stuck up a tree. Lots of men had come with a very long ladder and each time they got anywhere near him he had climbed even higher.

'Wheeeeeeeeeeeeeeee!' she squeaked. That would teach him not to try taking over from her.

She couldn't wait to tell Graham and Fangio. They liked stories with a happy ending too.

'You know, Olga,' said Karen Sawdust, as she gave her a final going over with the drier. 'There are times when I would give anything to be able to read what's in your mind.'

Perhaps, thought Olga, remembering what Mrs Sawdust had said only a few days before, it's lucky for me you can't!

7
Olga's Big Moment

One morning, long before the Sawdust family were awake, Olga was taking her usual early morning stroll round the living room, checking up on things while trying not to leave too many sawdust trails which might mean questions being asked, when something made her stop dead in her tracks.

She happened to be passing the French windows and as she glanced out she saw a

FACE looking straight at her. It was pressed hard against a pane of glass – a cracked one Mrs Sawdust was always talking about having replaced – and it was watching her every movement.

Worse still, as Olga slowly backed away it began licking its lips.

She turned on her heels and raced through her tunnels as fast as her legs would carry her. Although she had never actually met a fox before, she didn't need to be told what it was.

She clearly remembered a piece of advice an old guinea-pig in the pet shop had given the others when she was very small. 'When you go out into the world,' he'd said, 'as most of you surely will sooner or later, there are two things you need to look out for. The first one is foxes.'

He had certainly been right about going out into the world. A few days later Mr Sawdust brought Karen into the shop and they had taken her home to live with them, which was how she had come by her name.

She couldn't remember what the second

thing was she had been warned to look out for, but the thought of meeting a fox face to face had always stayed in her mind. According to the old guinea-pig, they ate anything they could get their teeth into and when they were hungry they let nothing stand in their way.

Olga hoped they weren't able to get their teeth into glass, and much to her relief, when she reached the safety of her own house and peered out through a gap in the hay, the face at the window had gone.

In fact, everything was so quiet she soon began to wonder if it hadn't all been part of a bad dream.

But when the Sawdust family came downstairs to breakfast, Mrs Sawdust could talk of nothing else.

'Fancy seeing a fox in our garden,' she said. 'Who would have thought it? Sitting in the middle of the lawn as large as life, staring at Graham's house. The cheek of it!'

'You don't think it was a large cat?' suggested Mr Sawdust. 'Or a dog?'

'It was a fox all right,' said Mrs Sawdust. 'As soon as I opened the bathroom window it ran off, but I could smell where it had been. It's Graham I'm worried about. It explains why I found his bedding strewn over the lawn the other morning. There were bits of it everywhere.'

'I shouldn't worry too much about Graham,' said Mr Sawdust. 'A fox would need to be pretty desperate before it tried sinking its teeth into him. His shell must be as hard as iron by now. He's had it long enough.'

'You never know,' said Karen. 'Graham might have gone to bed and left one of his legs sticking out. You know how forgetful he is. I don't suppose he knows himself where they are half the time. He probably doesn't even bother to count them before he goes to sleep.'

'Two things are certain sure,' said Mrs Sawdust. 'Olga mustn't go out on the lawn for the time being. *And* we must get that cracked pane of glass in the French windows replaced. You never know! One good tap with a fox's paw and he would be in the house like a shot.'

Olga was pleased to hear about the last two things. Much as she liked going outside in her run, she didn't fancy meeting the fox again with only the wire netting to protect her. As for the glass; she remembered the second thing the old pig had said. 'If you happen to be sitting by a window, always make sure it's properly closed. You never know what might come in!' Although a cracked pane of glass was better than nothing at all, it was nice to know it was going to be mended.

Mr Sawdust poured himself a second cup of coffee. 'Well, I think you're all making a fuss about nothing,' he said. 'There's a place for everything in this world and everything has its place. That includes foxes. I rather like the look of them myself. They have nice bushy tails.'

All the same, as soon as breakfast was over he went into the garden. He said he needed a bit of fresh air, but from the safety of her box Olga could see he went straight to Graham's house and lifted the lid to make sure he was all right.

After that he disappeared into the shrubbery and began looking around.

Olga thought she heard a cry, and sure enough, a few moments later Mr Sawdust reappeared. He had a face like thunder, and as he came back down the garden he appeared to be limping.

'You won't believe this!' he cried, as he entered the house. 'But that fox of yours has dug a blessed great hole in the middle of the shrubbery. Just look at the state of my trousers! I went in up to my knees.'

'Oh, dear,' said Mrs Sawdust. 'I hope Fangio doesn't fall into it. He's very accident prone.'

'Show me a hedgehog that isn't,' said Mr Sawdust. 'Anyway, what about me?'

'You're the one who said how much you like foxes!' said Mrs Sawdust.

'There are foxes and there are foxes,' said Mr Sawdust stiffly. 'Apart from digging a hole, this one has trodden all over the flowers. They're as flat as a pancake. I don't care what anyone says. We shall have to do something before it takes over.'

Mr Sawdust was unusually late back from his office that evening, and when he arrived home he went straight out into the garden carrying a cardboard box and some tools.

Watching through the window Olga saw him fixing a black object to the side of the summer house. As soon as he had finished work he pressed a button and it started making a whistling noise.

'There . . . that should fix it!' he exclaimed, as he came back indoors looking very pleased with himself.

He held up the empty box. 'I've been asking

around and this is the latest thing. It makes a noise that only animals can hear and it drives them potty. It says on the label that it's been tried and tested in the African jungle. Look . . . there's a picture of an elephant. If it works on elephants it ought to work on foxes . . . '

He broke off as there was a bang from the pussy flap and Noel came in from the garden looking cross about something.

'How do you know ours is working?' asked Mrs Sawdust.

'You'll see,' said Mr Sawdust.

'It's working all right,' Noel murmured darkly as he slunk past Olga. 'I can't hear myself think and Graham says the noise has given him a headache already.'

Olga could see what Noel meant. The whistling noise seemed to be everywhere. It came through the windows, it came through the doors, it even came through the outside walls and it felt as if it was going through her too; in one ear and out the other side! There was no stopping it.

She could still hear it long after the others had gone to bed. If anything, it sounded worse than ever after dark when everything else was quiet.

It was also true what it said on the box – it didn't seem to bother the Sawdust family at all. They went about the house as though nothing unusual was happening.

In the end it was Mrs Sawdust who first noticed the effect it was having on the animals.

'Graham hasn't been out of his house for days,' she said at dinner one night. 'I caught Noel with his head buried under a cushion this morning, and I've never known Olga be so quiet. She doesn't even squeak when she hears me open the refrigerator door.'

'It's not all bad then,' said Mr Sawdust. 'We must be thankful for small mercies.'

But he didn't really mean it, and a few mornings later when he looked out of the window and saw the fox on the lawn again he had to admit defeat. 'Just my luck,' he grumbled. 'I would have to pick on one that's as deaf as a post! I suppose we call out the hunt.'

'Is there one?' asked Mrs Sawdust.

'It was only a joke,' said Mr Sawdust wearily. 'But I'm not giving up. I've got other ideas up my sleeve.'

The very next evening he came home from the office carrying a large can and a brush. Once again he went straight out into the garden, but he was gone rather longer this time and when he eventually came indoors Olga heard a commotion.

Karen Sawdust looked up from her homework. 'Pooh!' she exclaimed. 'Is that it?'

'We shall lose all our friends,' said Mrs Sawdust, holding a handkerchief to her nose. 'I don't know about the fox, but nobody else will want to come and see us.'

'It'll be worth it in the end,' said Mr Sawdust. 'You mark my words. The man in the shop said if it doesn't do the trick, nothing will. I've painted all what he called "the surrounding areas". Just you wait!'

'Pooh!' was more or less what the man who came to repair the window said the next morning. He only stayed a few minutes, and the smell indoors was even worse after he had gone. Olga had a job finishing her breakfast it was so bad.

With Mr Sawdust away at the office, Karen at school, and Mrs Sawdust out shopping she was on her own for a while and she felt very hard done by. She supposed it might have been worse. She might still have been living outside in the garden instead of in the house, exposed to the fox, but all the same . . .

She looked up at that point and her eyes grew round. Talk of the devil – there it was again! That same evil face was staring at her through the French windows. Thank goodness the man had been to mend it. Plucking up her courage she stared straight back.

'Wheee!' she cried. 'It's all your fault!'

Having run round and round in circles several times she ended up back at the window, but even closer this time.

'Wheeeeee! You've upset Graham. He's been having nightmares ever since he woke up and found his bedding gone. Wheeeeeeeeeee!

And I'm not allowed to go out in the garden any more so I haven't seen Fangio for days.'

She did two more circles round the room and this time ended up only a whisker's length away from the window.

'Wheeeeeeeeeeeeeeee!' she cried. '*And* I'll have you know Noel's frightened to go out after dark. Wheeeeeeeeeeeeeeeeeeeeeeee! *And* Mr Sawdust fell down one of your holes. Wheeeeeeeeeeeeeeeeeeeeeeeeeeeeee ! *And . . .*' Olga paused for breath.

Suddenly realizing the fox was no longer there, she went back to her house for a much needed snack, quite worn out by it all.

'Well!' said Noel as he came back into the room. 'I wouldn't have believed it if I hadn't seen it with my own eyes.'

Wondering for a moment what he was talking about, Olga took a quick nibble of her oats. 'It was nothing,' she said.

'Nothing?' repeated Noel. '*Nothing?* I don't call chasing a fox off nothing. I think what you did was the bravest thing I've ever seen.'

101

'I suppose it's different if you're a cat,' said Olga carelessly. 'But it's the kind of thing we guinea-pigs do all the time. Only we don't go on about it, of course.'

'That's all very well,' said Noel. 'I could understand it if the man had been back to put the new glass in the window, instead of leaving a hole. But to face a fox like that, with *nothing* between you. Well, that takes some doing. It's a wonder it didn't have you for breakfast. Wait until the others hear.'

Olga felt her blood run cold and her legs turned to jelly.

'Where are you going?' asked Noel.

'I think I may have a lie down for a while,' said Olga weakly as she crawled back into her hay. 'I'm not feeling very well!'

The man who was repairing the window came and fitted a new piece of glass, then he went away again. It was hard to tell if Olga heard him or not.

Noel sat watching her house for a while. But when nothing stirred, he gave up, and having

102

made sure the coast was clear, he went outside to look for Graham and Fangio.

Olga didn't emerge from her hay until it was time for lunch, and even then she dragged each piece separately into her house before she ate it.

It would be a long time before she looked out into the garden again in case she saw another face at the window.

8

Tunnel Trouble

Mr Sawdust sat bolt upright up in bed. 'Did you hear that?' he exclaimed. 'Did you hear it?'

'It's only Olga, dear,' said Mrs Sawdust sleepily.

'Only Olga!' repeated Mr Sawdust, as another long-drawn-out, rasping sound echoed round the room. '*Only Olga!* It sounds as though someone's run amok with a tree saw!'

'She enjoys her paper tearing,' said Mrs Sawdust. 'It gives her something to do.'

'If she's looking for something to do,' said Mr Sawdust crossly, 'I'm not short of ideas. And she can find somewhere else to do it as well!' He reached for the light switch. 'If you ask me she only does it to attract attention. It's bad enough when she's being kept waiting for her breakfast and starts clinking her bowls. I don't see why she can't go in with Karen. She's her pig after all.'

'You know very well why,' said Mrs Sawdust. 'Karen's got her end of term exams. She needs all the sleep she can get.'

'And I suppose I don't,' snorted Mr Sawdust. 'If Olga wants to practise her origami at half past three in the morning she'd better go back downstairs.'

'She can't do that either,' said Mrs Sawdust firmly. 'The decorators haven't finished yet, and you know how the smell of fresh paint upsets her.'

'In that case,' said Mr Sawdust, clutching at straws, 'we'll put her in the boxroom.'

'Certainly not,' said Mrs Sawdust decidedly. 'It's much too cold in there.'

'Well, it's either her or me,' said Mr Sawdust.

Mrs Sawdust gave a yawn and turned over.

'There's a spare duvet in the toy cupboard,' she said. 'But don't say I didn't warn you.'

From the safety of her box in the corner of the bedroom Olga tried hard to ignore the voices. She didn't know what the problem was, but she hoped it would soon go away. It was all very well, but she couldn't concentrate on what she was doing with all the noise. It was worse than the television.

She didn't know what had woken her. Hunger, she supposed.

It had been a moment or two before she remembered where she was, and her first thought had been to stock up from her seed bowl. Finding it empty, she'd had to make do with paper.

Not that she minded. Provided it was nice and soft, there was a lot to be said for paper. There had been those in the pet shop where she had first started life who said it was good for you. All were agreed that it didn't do you any harm, although most of them avoided the shiny sort that got stuck in your teeth.

Olga also liked the sound paper made when

it was being torn into strips. Practice makes perfect, and she had it off to a fine art. In fact, the noise she made was very similar to that made by the others when they were cleaning her out and had to tear the ends off newspapers so that they would fit the bottom of her house. The only difference was that by doing it slowly she was able to make hers last much longer.

Anyway, she reasoned, if the Sawdust people didn't like the sound of it, why put newspaper in the bottom of her house in the first place? It was asking for trouble.

Gradually, as her eyes grew used to the light, everything came back to her. Where she was, how she had got there, and most of all why she was in Mr and Mrs Sawdust's bedroom at all.

It was because they were having their downstairs rooms decorated, and since there wasn't long to go before Christmas it needed to be done as quickly as possible, so for the time being everything in the house had been moved around.

In a roundabout way Olga herself had been partly responsible.

It all began when some people called 'relations' came to stay. They hadn't been there many days before one called 'Uncle Roger' got up from the table after dinner, pushed his chair back without looking, and squashed one of her tunnels against the skirting board. Luckily she hadn't been inside it, and at the time no one, least of all Uncle Roger, noticed what had happened.

It wasn't until the following day, when she was doing her early morning rounds and heard someone coming down the stairs, that she discovered the truth.

Racing into it in order to get back home as quickly as possible, she came to a sudden halt as she found herself stuck halfway; unable to go forward and too frightened to back out again.

And that hadn't been the worst of it. When

Mr Sawdust saw the tunnel moving around the room, seemingly all by itself, he picked it up while she was still inside and only just managed to catch her in time when she fell out.

It was hard to say who was more surprised, Olga or Mr Sawdust.

Olga was very fond of her tunnels. Mr Sawdust had made them especially for her out of some old champagne bottle cartons, and although the cardboard was very strong, it wasn't meant for that kind of treatment.

She didn't go near them again until some days after the guests had left, and even then Mrs Sawdust caught her coming out of the spare room, where she had been to make doubly certain Uncle Roger really had gone for good.

It was while Mrs Sawdust had been crawling around on her hands and knees trying to find Olga that she decided both rooms were badly in need of decorating.

The dining room was the last to be done, which was how she found herself spending the night in a strange room.

Having worked all that out in her mind she was about to settle down again when she felt her house rising up into the air and a moment later it began jiggling up, down, and every which way, like a ship at sea.

'Make sure she's got plenty of hay,' called Mrs Sawdust. 'And don't forget her water bowl. I should leave the door open in case she wonders where she is in the night and calls out.'

But Olga didn't need to be told. As soon as Mr Sawdust put her house back down on the floor and she was able to look out, she knew exactly where she had been taken.

Although it was a room she had never been into before, it was easy to see how it had got its name. There were boxes everywhere. Large ones, middle size ones, small ones: she had never seen so many; all piled higgledy-piggledy on top of each other.

In one corner, separate from the rest, there was a pile of brightly coloured parcels. They looked very familiar, but try as she might she couldn't remember where or when she had seen them before.

While Mr Sawdust went downstairs to fetch a fresh supply of hay, Olga poked her head out further still and gave a shiver. Mrs Sawdust was right when she said the room would be cold. It had a different smell to it too; not a nasty one, but more as though there was something extra in the air. Something special.

Venturing even further out of her house, Olga peered round the room and gave another sniff. Suddenly, she realized what it was. In a far corner, behind a bed, there were some newspapers. Not just a small pile like the one that was kept for her special use downstairs, and which came and went, but a huge mound made up of several piles, which seemed to go on and on until they met halfway up the wall.

She felt herself begin to drool. Old newspapers were even nicer than new ones. For a start, old newspapers didn't taste of ink like new ones sometimes did. Mrs Sawdust often complained about the way the ink rubbed off and made her tablecloths dirty.

Olga couldn't wait for Mr Sawdust to get back with her hay, and as soon as he had said goodnight and switched out the overhead light she set to work.

First of all she made a barrier across the front part of her house in order to keep out the draught. Then, with the hay that was left over, she started building a nest.

If there was one thing above all else that Olga was good at, it was making herself comfortable. Karen Sawdust often said she wouldn't mind sharing her bed, although she never did, of course, because there wasn't room

for two. Mr Sawdust, on the other hand, maintained that the way Olga went about arranging her hay was better than having a barometer, for when it promised to be warm she always spread it neatly and thinly over the floor of her house, whereas when it was going to be cold she fluffed it all up so that it became twice the size.

As soon as she was satisfied, Olga stopped work, pricked up her ears to make sure that all was quiet, then set off in the moonlight to explore her new surroundings.

She knew where she was heading, but she couldn't resist having a look at the parcels first.

From a distance they had looked very interesting; close to they were even more so. Each one had a small piece of cardboard dangling from it, and in every case when she gave it a tug it came away.

It didn't take Olga long to finish them off. Pleased with her handiwork, she set off towards the mound of newspapers.

Just as she had thought, there was a small passageway in the middle where two of the piles didn't quite meet. It felt just like entering one

of her own tunnels, and without a second thought she made her way inside. It was smaller than she had expected, but she soon found herself in a much bigger space, not unlike a tiny room; big enough for her to turn round so that she could face the way she had come.

Another nice thing about tunnels was the safe feeling they gave of being hidden from the rest of the world, yet still able to see light at either end and hear what was going on.

Feeling something tickling the end of her nose Olga looked up. To her surprise a loose piece of newspaper fell straight into her open mouth. It was like a dream come true!

Taking it between her teeth she gave a tug.

When nothing happened she took a firmer grip and tried again, but still nothing happened, so she decided to have one last go.

Leaning back and digging her feet into the carpet Olga gave a third and final tug. She immediately wished she hadn't, as there was a slithering and sliding noise from somewhere overhead and everything suddenly went dark.

'Wheeeeeeeeeeeeeeeeeeeeeeeeeeeeeeeeeeee!'
she cried.

It should have been one of the loudest and longest squeaks she had ever made, but even to her ears it sounded strangely muffled. Deep inside her Olga knew that the chances of anyone else hearing it were very small indeed.

For a long while she lay where she was, hardly daring to breathe in case it made matters worse. In the end she decided there was only one thing for it. Inching herself forward until she felt something touch the end of her nose again, she took a tiny nibble this time. She held her breath for a moment or two, and when nothing happened carefully took a second nibble, then a third, before starting work in earnest.

It was a very long time before Olga saw the light at the end of the tunnel. By then it was much brighter than it had been when she first went inside, for the sun was now streaming in through the boxroom window, but she was much too tired to care one way or the other.

And as with the time when she had nearly fallen out of her cardboard tunnel, it was hard to tell who was the more relieved when Mr Sawdust found her.

'Thank goodness,' said Mrs Sawdust, when she arrived in answer to his call. She bent down and picked Olga up. 'We've been looking for you everywhere. You were nowhere to be seen when we came in this morning.'

Mr Sawdust looked at the pile of fallen newspapers. 'Fancy her being in there all the time,' he said. 'She must have eaten her way out. But if that's the case, what happened to all the bits?'

'Feel her stomach,' said Mrs Sawdust. 'It's as tight as a drum.'

'A girl has to do what a girl has to do,' said Karen, taking Olga from her mother.

Olga snuggled up and gave a long purr of delight at the sound of all the familiar voices. There had been a moment when she thought she might never hear them again.

Mr Sawdust reached out. 'May I have a go?'

'There! Did you feel that?' he exclaimed, as Olga dug her toes into Karen's watch strap and took a flying leap into his open hands. 'Those back legs of hers are like two tightly coiled springs. *And* she has total trust that someone will catch her. What with that and her origami she really ought to join a circus.' He held her high up in the air for the others to see. 'Who's a daring young girl on the flying trapeze, then?'

I'm not for a start, thought Olga, as she swooped back down again. She had no idea what a trapeze was, but if daring meant what she thought it meant, it was the last thing she wanted to be, especially on a full stomach.

'If you ask me,' said Mrs Sawdust, 'I think we had better try having Olga in with us again tonight. I don't think she'll be doing any paper-tearing again for a while.'

Mr Sawdust looked disappointed. 'Oh dear,' he said. 'Do you think so? I was hoping she would. It's rather a nice sound. I was looking forward to hearing it again!'

Olga gazed up at his face. She had said it before, and she would say it again. There was no telling with Sawdust people what they liked and what they didn't like.

It really was most confusing at times!

ENDPIECE

The Sawdust family never knew why they didn't see the fox again.

Mr Sawdust was sure it was because of the smell, and it was certainly a fact that for a while a lot of people stopped coming to see them.

But there were others who knew the truth. Graham, Fangio, and even Noel, spoke with pride of the part Olga had played. Her fame spread, and the more it spread the greater the tale became, until it wasn't just one fox, but a whole pack she had put to flight.

As for Olga herself, she was too much of a lady to argue the point. For once in her life she had nothing more to say on the subject, although for a long time afterwards she couldn't look at the window without feeling her legs turn to jelly.

The heron never came near the Sawdust family's garden again either, although it was seen more than once in the neighbourhood.

Venables, the toad, went into hibernation in the middle of October, but because of the change in the weather pattern Graham and Fangio were later than usual. Fangio was the first to disappear, but it was early November before Mrs Sawdust caught Graham digging himself in under the wall at the end of the garden. She promptly rescued him before he disappeared altogether; there was always a danger of there being a hard frost.

She brought out her scales (he weighed 1,770 grams) and afterwards put him to bed under some straw in the summer house for safe keeping.

Then, one morning, not long after her adventure with the tunnel, Olga woke to find all the parcels she had seen in the boxroom spread out on the dining room table.

She realized why they had looked so familiar. They were Christmas presents!

At first there was some confusion as to who they were meant for. Mrs Sawdust swore she'd been very careful to label them all, but everyone else said she couldn't have – if she had, where were they? And in the general excitement it was soon forgotten.

All the same, Olga kept quiet while they were being opened in case they put two and two together, but she appeared in time to find Mr Sawdust had made her a new tunnel to replace the one that had got squashed!

It was the nicest present she could remember having for a long time, and she spent most of the afternoon asleep in it.

Noel had a tin of his favourite cat food, so after lunch he went to sleep too.

By the time Olga woke it was starting to get dark.

Mr Sawdust gave her some champagne to sniff but it tickled the end of her nose so she turned her back on it. In any case Mrs Sawdust thought it might make her slur her squeaks. Olga didn't like the sound of that, but it was nice to feel part of the family and to know that they cared.

For the first time in ages she plucked up courage and made her way to the French windows. It looked very cold outside and when she got close a tiny patch of mist appeared on the glass just beyond the end of her nose, which made her feel better.

It was hard to picture Graham and Fangio out there still fast asleep; missing all those meals, and Christmas too.

'Wheeeeeeeeeee!' She tried giving them a squeak, but nothing moved.

She would have a lot to tell them when they woke up, but in the meantime there was a lot to be said for being a guinea-pig and living with the Sawdust family .

It was such a nice thought, Olga turned and went back to her house. And in her house, between nibbles from her bowl of oats, she thought it all over again.

MICHAEL BOND (1926-2017) grew up in Reading, England, along with a dog called Binkie and three guinea-pigs named Pip, Squeak, and Wilfred. He began writing in 1947 while serving with the army in Egypt. Short stories and radio plays followed, but it wasn't until 1958 that his first children's book, *A Bear Called Paddington*, was published. The phenomenally successful 'Paddington' books eventually led him to give up working as a BBC television cameraman in order to write full time. Inspired by his daughter Karen's guinea-pig, he embarked on the 'Olga da Polga' series, which has now been adapted for television. Michael Bond was honoured with an OBE in 1997 for his services to children's literature and a CBE in 2015.

OTHER OLGA DA POLGA BOOKS

The Tales of Olga da Polga

ISBN: 978-0-19-278753-8

From the very beginning there was not the slightest doubt that Olga da Polga was the sort of guinea-pig who would go places.

Olga da Polga is no ordinary guinea-pig. From the rosettes in her fur to her unusual name, there's something special about her . . . and Olga knows it!

Olga has a wild imagination, and from the minute she arrives at her new home, she begins entertaining all the other animals in the garden with her outrageous tales and stories—but she still has time to get up to all kinds of mischief and have lots of wonderful adventures too.

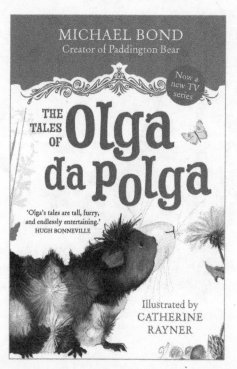

MICHAEL BOND
Creator of Paddington Bear

Now a new TV series

Olga
Meets Her Match

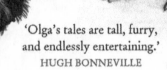

'Olga's tales are tall, furry, and endlessly entertaining.'
HUGH BONNEVILLE

Olga Meets Her Match

ISBN: 978-0-19-278747-7

Just in front of her there was an opening in the wall of the main building which she hadn't noticed before, and standing barely a whisker's length away in the darkness beyond was another guinea-pig. For a moment . . . neither of them spoke, and then the other stirred.

'You must be Olga,' he said. 'I was told you were coming.'

Olga da Polga goes visiting and meets Boris, a Russian guinea-pig. Olga and Boris become firm friends and Olga is surprised to discover that Boris can tell even taller tales than she can! Soon the time comes for her to return to her own garden, but Olga doesn't mind, she can't wait to tell the other animals all about her trip and, of course, her new friend, and she even gives them all a demonstration of her Russian dancing skills . . .

MICHAEL BOND
Creator of Paddington Bear

Now a new TV series

Olga
Carries On

'Olga's tales
are tall, furry,
and endlessly
entertaining.'
HUGH BONNEVILLE

Olga Carries On

ISBN: 978-0-19-278743-9

Olga suddenly decided she liked the newcomers after all. Anyone who was so small and yet could stick up for himself and bite someone hundreds of times his own size must have some good in him. She decided to get in first.

'Wheeeeeeeeeee!' she squeaked. 'Welcome to the family.'

Fircone and Raisin are the new arrivals in the Sawdust family and Olga is delighted to see them. After all, they're just in time to hear her first attempts at poetry and listen to her plan to find out who has been raiding the Sawdust's kitchen. She might even find time to tell them a brand new story . . .

MICHAEL BOND
Creator of Paddington Bear

Now a new TV series

Olga
Takes charge

'Olga's tales are tall, furry, and endlessly entertaining.'
HUGH BONNEVILLE

Olga Takes Charge

ISBN: 978-0-19-278751-4

Olga was in a jam. In fact, that day she had been in a number of different jams, each worse than the one before, until her mind was in such a whirl she didn't know which way to turn.

Olga is a very busy guinea-pig. She attempts to save the Sawdust family from the effects of a drought, she participates in a sponsored squeak, and she even takes up jogging. But somehow she always manages to find time to delight her friends with her tall tales and far-fetched stories.

MICHAEL BOND
Creator of Paddington Bear

Now a
new TV
series

Olga
Moves House

'Olga's tales are tall, furry, and endlessly
entertaining.' HUGH BONNEVILLE

Olga Moves House

ISBN: 978-0-19-278749-1

No one in the Sawdust family could remember exactly when it happened, but happen it did. One moment Olga was living in her hutch in the garden, the next moment she had moved into their house. Once there, she made herself very much at home in a corner of the dining room; as large as life 'thank you very much', and often—especially when it was getting near meal times—twice as noisy.

Winter has come to the Sawdust household, and Olga's been moved into a new home, inside the house. She's very excited about her new home and has even managed to get Mrs Sawdust to do a spot of redecorating! Olga enjoys watching the comings and goings inside the house and still manages to get herself into mischief whilst embarking on many wonderful adventures.

'Olga's tales are tall, furry,
and endlessly entertaining.'
HUGH BONNEVILLE